My Slut

I made her my own, my slave

Series: Lesbian a Taboo Family Secret Story

Collection Taboo Sex Erotica

By Marguerite de Lyon

Copyright © 2015 Marguerite de Lyon

ISBN-13: 978-1512239218 ISBN-10: 1512239216

Contents

CHAPTER ONE: A New Arrival 1

CHAPTER TWO: An Evening Of Discovery 7

CHAPTER THREE: Going Deeper.. 27

CHAPTER FOUR: The Ultimate Fantasy............................... 33

Collection Taboo Sex Erotica.. 44

The Author... 45

Chapter One: A New Arrival

I got my first look at her from across the office. It's an open plan space, and so all I had to do was stand up and I could see over all the desks and dividers and pot plants to where she stood by the reception desk. She looked nothing like I had expected her to. Nothing like anybody had described. She was so... prim. That was what surprised me about her.

Her name was Sandy, and she was to be the newest member of the sales department. I work at a company that sells advertising space in a bunch of different magazines. The sales department is one of the hardest departments to work in. The pressure is huge, the deadlines short and the expectations high. The rewards are pretty great too, but you have to be something special to work in sales. You have to be... tough, I guess. And Sandy did not look tough.

Sandy, in fact, looked soft. Girlish. She was wearing a light pink blouse and a neat black skirt, and she carried her folder full of papers in front of her. Her blonde hair was done up in a ponytail that reached all the way down to the small of her back, and her eyes were accentuated by a pair of purple-rimmed glasses. Looking at her you'd be forgiven for thinking she'd stepped right out of university.

Inwardly, I groaned. This was always happening. In the interests of diversity, they were always hiring women to work in sales. Unfortunately most of them left after only a week or two. The environment was too high-pressure for them, and they couldn't take it. It looked as though Sandy was set to be the next in a long line of failures.

Still, at least she was pretty, I consoled myself. As the only other woman in the department it would almost certainly fall to me to show her the ropes. Thus we'd be spending an awful lot of time in one another's company over the next few weeks. At least I'd have something pleasant to look at while I was helping her.

I shuffled some papers on my desk, and watched as Sandy was shown across the office to the corner dedicated to sales. The receptionist shot me a look as they approached, and I nodded and rolled my eyes, before stepping forward to introduce myself.

"Hi there. My name's Dinah. And you must be Sandy. I'll be showing you around." I held out my hand for her to shake, and she gripped it with surprising firmness, while at the same time performing something akin to a curtsey. I had to stifle the urge to laugh. Someone as innocent and feminine as her wouldn't last two weeks in this place. Ah, well...

"Please to meet you," said Sandy, smiling. "I heard a lot about you during my interview."

I raised my eyebrows. "Really? All good, I hope?"

"Mostly," said Sandy, and I swear she almost winked at me. Hmm. Interesting. Perhaps I'd have to revise my opinion of her once I'd gotten to know her a little bit better. Time for that later though. I gestured for her to follow me, and we set off on a tour around the office.

*

Sandy surprised me a couple of times that afternoon. To start with, she held her own in a conversation with Giles from the marketing department. Giles is one of those guys who automatically thinks of themselves as the alpha male of whatever group they happen to find themselves in – which is really just a convoluted way of saying that he's an obnoxious prick. More often than not if you introduce him to a woman, she won't get a word in edgeways during the conversation that ensues. Not so with Sandy.

Giles had just launched into his usual speil about how he'd been working at the office for ages, and how she could come and speak to him anytime if she had any problems, and Sandy was nodding and smiling and simpering along, just as I'd expected her to. I watched her, enjoying having my first impression of her confirmed. But then, seemingly from nowhere, she held up a hand and cocked her head. It looked as though she'd just heard something that the two of us had missed. Giles stopped mid-flow, and even I couldn't help but turn to her, intrigued as to what she was about to say. A moment later the look dropped from her face and she was smiling again.

"I do apologise," she said, "but Dinah's in the middle of showing me around. We'll have to continue this conversation another time." And with that we were off again, continuing on our way. I shook my head in admiration. It was, I had to admit, a masterful was of dealing with a man like Giles.

Sandy was, as it turned out, surprisingly good at handling people. I watched her closely through her first few sales calls. After starting out with the scripted pitch and getting shot down a couple of times, she very quickly started to modify it – giving her name and making some small talk before saying why she was calling, as well as using people's names. I'd never seen a new hire adjust so quickly before. It really was a marvel.

I would never, under normal circumstances, have invited a new girl out for drinks after work. But Sandy was different. What can I say? She impressed me. And so come six o' clock, when everyone else was heading home, me and her made our way down the road to the nearest friendly pub – a quiet little place with its entrance just inside the mouth of an alleyway. I bought her a drink, and we settled ourselves at the back of the room.

"I have to say," I said. "I was kind of impressed by the way you handled yourself today. Most new people aren't so... good."

Sandy laughed graciously and swept her hair behind her ear. I found myself staring at the curve of her neck. Everything about her was so incredibly pretty – and yet you could tell that she was smart too. More than just an empty vessel. I shook myself, and tuned back in to what she was saying.

"I'm just adaptable," she said. "I've learned how to fit in. How to handle people. Really, I guess, I'm a people pleaser. That's all I want – to do well. To please. And learning how to conduct myself – I suppose that's part of it."

I nodded, satisfied with her answer. We drank our drinks and settled quickly to chatting about more normal things. What she did outside of work. Friends. Family. I learned that she was relatively new to London, but that she'd settled in well. No boyfriend or girlfriend, though she attracted plenty of interest, it seemed, from the number of dates she went on. Living in a little flat up in Hackney. She seemed to have it pretty much together.

"And why have none of these dates been successful?" I asked, smiling to soften the question. I was curious, I had to admit. She was cute, articulate and her body was amazing. I could hardly believe that she hadn't been snapped up already. In answer to my question Sandy shrugged and sighed.

"I don't know," she said. "All the people were very nice, very lovely. But they just didn't... excite me, do you know what I mean? There was just something missing."

I nodded sympathetically. I'd had that feeling before – in fact, I knew it all too well. Part of me, however, noted the fact that she was single, and that she seemed to date both men and women. It seemed almost too good to be true to imagine that I might be able to seduce her. But... well, it was at least worth a try. I decided then and there that I would do my best to make Sandy mine before the end of the year.

"What about you," said Sandy, casually. "How's your love life going? You got a boyfriend?"

I smiled indulgently. "Oh," I said with a smile, "several."

Sandy looked surprised only for a moment. "Several?" she said. "You mean..." She left the question hanging in the air.

I debated with myself for a moment as to how truthful I wanted to be with her. I could tell her everything, but it might – of course – put her off me entirely. She struck me as someone who was probably pretty vanilla, but then my very first impression of her had already been proved wrong. Perhaps I was mistaken about that as well. Perhaps, were I to divulge some of the more interesting secrets of my sex life to her, she might even be intrigued.

For a moment or two I stared at my drink in silence, weighing up my possible courses of action. And then – perhaps because I was a little tipsy from the beer – I made my decision. I would tell her as much as she wanted to know. Perhaps she would like what she heard, but even if she didn't I felt reasonably confident in my ability to corrupt her.

"Well," I said, "I wouldn't say that they were all boyfriends, exactly. Some of them are more like slaves. Submissives, you might call them. My subs."

Sandy's eyes were wide and round, and I drank in the expression of amazement written across her features. "So... so you... dominate them?" she said. "Does that mean that you're a-"

"A domme," I said. "That's right."

For a moment Sandy simply stared at me over the top of her pint glass. I held my breath, wondering what she was going to say next. Would she slam down her glass and flounce out in disgust? If so, the next few weeks would almost certainly be terribly awkward. Or would she lean forwards, brush her hair behind her ear and ask me to tell her more.

After a tense pause, and much to my relief, it turned out to be the second one. "So what kind of things do you do to them?" asked Sandy, her voice hushed.

"All sorts. It depends what they're into," I said. I didn't lower my voice at all. I wanted Sandy to know that I was quite happy to talk about these things, quite comfortable with this part of my life. "I whip them sometimes, or I torture them with hot wax and needles. I tie them up. I make them worship me." I shrugged casually. "Depends on my mood as well, a lot of the time." I couldn't help laughing at how surprised Sandy looked. Her mouth was hanging open, and she seemed to have entirely forgotten the drink in front of her. She saw me smiling, and gathered herself.

"That's really... interesting," she said. She swirled her drink around in its glass. "I suppose I've always been interested in that kind of stuff," she said. "Always been curious. I've just never had anyone to explore it with."

It was almost too good to be true. No sooner had I decided that I wanted Sandy, then she decided to basically present herself on a plate for me. So long as I was careful, I could surely make my fantasies come true.

"Well," I said carefully. "You'd be welcome to drop by my place sometime. I'd be more than willing to help you... explore."

For a moment Sandy looked surprised, but she recovered quickly. She took a sip of her beer, then set the glass down again. She swept her hair behind her ear. "Is that a serious offer," she said.

"Absolutely serious," I replied.

She nodded her head, deep in thought. Then she looked directly at me, her eyes wide but piercing nonetheless. "I'd love to," she said. "In fact, I can hardly wait."

Chapter Two: An Evening Of Discovery

We decided between us that we wouldn't do anything that night, and that we'd wait until tomorrow for Sandy to accompany me home after work. In part this was because I wanted to give her some cooling off time, and in part it was because – if I was going to play with someone as attractive as her – I wanted a little bit of time to get myself ready first.

That evening was spent preparing for the following day. I took a long bath, washed my hair, moisturised my skin and clipped my nails. I took my box of toys out of the cupboard and made sure that they were clean. I washed my bedsheets and I picked out an outfit for tomorrow – something that would be okay to wear for work, but that might also get Sandy's juices flowing.

And all the while as I was doing this I found myself thinking of her. I couldn't stop obsessing over her blonde hair, her neat little body, her perfectly-sized breasts, each one of which looked like it was just the right size for me to cup in my hand. Little things about her seemed to have stuck with me as well. I kept replaying in my head the way her eyes had gone wide when I started talking about my sex life, or the graceful way she'd lifted her glass to her lips. Oh, she was perfect. I could hardly wait to get my hands on her.

But, unfortunately, waiting was exactly what I would have to do. It took me ages to fall asleep that night, and I woke up early the next morning. I showered meticulously, and took a few moments to shave off the few hairs that I found on my body. I wanted to be smooth and perfect for her. I wanted my body to impress her, maybe even intimidate her with its perfection. I moisturised myself, plucked my eyebrows and painted my nails. I even put on some makeup, which is a thing I only do very rarely.

All in all, as I stepped into the office that day, I would have to admit that I looked far more fantastic than usual. The skirt and black top that I'd picked out were certainly attention-grabbing. I could feel eyes following me from every direction as I walked across to my desk. I didn't mind. They were more than welcome to look, of course, but the only person who would be permitted to do any more than that was Sandy.

And there was. I saw her, once again, from all the way across the office, and was gratified to notice that she'd put in every bit as much effort as I had. Her hair was tied back and featured a complicated little braid that ran around the top of her head like a crown. Her blouse today was showing some cleavage, and her legs were encased in sheer black tights beneath an intriguingly short skirt.

She'd been assigned a desk just across from me, and she walked up and took her seat with only the most casual of greetings. I could see in her eyes though that she was excited to see me, that she was checking me out.

The day proceeded as most days do. Slowly. It was made infinitely worse by the fact that Sandy was sitting not ten foot away from me, practically glowing with beauty. It was torture. Every time I walked past her desk I had to restrain myself from putting out a hand and gliding it along the smooth curve of her back. I longed to seize her, to hold her, push her down, dominate her, fuck her, make her mine. But, unfortunately, there was nothing I could do. Not until five o' clock, which seemed just then as though it was an age away.

As the day wore on though, visions of what Sandy and I might do that evening swam through my brain. I couldn't focus, couldn't settle to anything. If I was going to get any work done at all today something would have to be done. After a few minutes thought, an idea occurred to me. Perhaps it wouldn't be necessary to wait quite so long to have her after all. Perhaps, if we were careful, we might be able to make the day pass a little quicker.

"Sandy," I said, standing up. "Could you give me a hand with something?" I didn't wait for her to answer, but simply started walking towards the stairwell. I was her superior after all. I heard her hurrying after me, and increased my pace a little so that we reached the doors at the same time. Just as I had hoped she would, Sandy hopped forward and held the door for me. I smiled at her, and said in a voice so low that nobody else in the office would be able to hear, "Good girl."

Alone in the stairwell, the frisson between us intensified. But we couldn't do anything here. No. It was far too public – we'd almost certainly be discovered. We would need to find somewhere more private, and I knew just the place.

Up we went, our shoes clacking sharply on the steps. The document storage room was two floors up – it was where we kept archive copies of every magazine, newspaper and publication we had ever worked on. The space was huge, but it was a rare day that anyone had any excuse to go there. It was the perfect location for me to test Sandy for the very first time.

When we reached the store, Sandy held the door open for me again. It was dim inside – the lights were off and the blinds were drawn. She followed me in, peering around curiously at the stacks and shelves and boxes. To her credit though, she didn't ask a single question. Somehow she knew that this wasn't the time.

At the very back of the room, in a corner protected by a couple of huge metal shelving units, I turned to face her. It was quiet in the room, but not silent. You could hear the footsteps of people moving about on the floor above, and traffic noises coming in through an open window somewhere. Dust motes drifted in the air between us. My cunt throbbed.

"Sandy," I said. Her name hovered in the air between us. I stepped forward. She stepped forward too, so that we were standing almost nose to nose. "I don't want to wait until this evening," I said. "I'm an impatient woman."

Sandy swallowed audibly. "I... Um..." She opened her mouth, but didn't seem able to find the words. And so I spoke for her.

"Kiss me," I said. And, tentatively at first, she did. She brought her face close to mine and brushed her soft lips against mine. Her hand went to my waist, and I looped an arm around the small of her back, pulling her closer. Her hair tickled my cheek. Her breath bounced off my face. And then we were kissing, our lips locked, our tongues pressing against one another. She tasted divine, and she was so delicate in her every little movement.

I knew then that I would dominate her. However in control and capable she seemed, she wouldn't be able to stand up to me. I could feel it in the way her body melted a little against me, her grip going soft, her breath becoming short.

I pushed the kiss harder, allowing my tongue to explore her mouth thoroughly and completely. And then I brought my other hand up and ran it down the side of her neck, ever so lightly, ever so gently. She exhaled into me, and then gasped when I grabbed a handful of her breast through her blouse. I squeezed. They were ripe, soft and full and wonderful, heaving with her breath.

We broke apart. Sandy brushed her hair behind her ear. "Was that okay?" she said. "It's been a while since I kissed a woman."

I smiled. "That was wonderful," I said. "But now I want to see what else you can do with your mouth."

Sandy licked her lips, her eyes flicking from my eyes to my mouth and then down my body. I felt the power in that gaze. How she was drawn to me. Was this too much? Or was this exactly what she wanted. For a moment time stood still. Well, there was only one way to find out. I tried to keep my finger steady as I hitched up my skirt to reveal my black silken panties. They were already wet – had been from the moment that Sandy pressed her warm body against mine during the kiss. I hooked a finger into them and pulled them aside. With one hand I held my skirt and panties in place, and with the other I beckoned to Sandy to come closer.

She did so. I didn't even have to tell her to get on her knees, she simply sank down of her own accord and raised her hands as though she were about to take hold of my hips. At the last moment she stopped though and looked up towards me as though seeking permission. Seeing her like that, kneeling before me, her wide eyes directed upwards, sent a thrill of arousal through my body. I nodded my permission, and she placed her hands on my hips. My wet slit was in front of her face, only a few inches away. I tilted my hips so that it would be open for her, so that she could reach it with her tongue. She leaned forwards, knees together, slow and careful.

At first she only breathed on me. I could feel her warm breath shivering these against me, and it felt amazing. Then she kissed me. She kissed the crease of my thighs and my pubis and the lips of my cunt. Then she kissed me there. Right there. I groaned in pleasure. Her mouth was sweet and moist and hot and it felt so right just there, so absolutely right. Every inch of my skin tingled with pleasure as her lips moved against me.

"That's right," I murmured. "Good girl. Lick me. Make me feel good. Make me come. Oh, that's what need. That's what I want from you ."

And sure enough her tongue soon came into play. She licked me in long strokes at first, from my wet hole all the way up to my clit. The feel of her tongue against that most sensitive part of me made me want to writhe in pleasure, but I held myself steady so that she could continue her ministrations. Her hands were tight on my hips, pulling me into her, and she quickly picked up pace, licking and tonguing me eagerly. My juices lacquered her face, filled her mouth. The thought that she could taste me filled me with a sense of pure and absolute joy.

"Come on, slut," I whispered. "Harder. Lick me harder. Put your fingers inside of me. I want you to make me come here and now."

Obediently, Sandy removed one hand from my hip and gently slid two fingers up inside me. I was so well-lubricated with my own intimate fluids that her fingers slid in smoothly. I felt her crook them inside me and start to stroke, all the while still licking at me. She was focussed on my clit now, massaging it with her tongue, making circles around it with the tip. She was amazing, by far the best I'd had in ages. I stole a glance down at her, on her knees before me, giving everything to make me feel good. And doing so still fully clothed, still wearing the clothes she'd strolled into the office with that morning. It all felt somehow secret and special and covert.

I could feel my orgasm building. I wound a hand into Sandy's hair, just behind the braid and pushed her a little harder against my crotch. She responded in kind, increasing the pace of her licking. She was making little noises, moans and groans of pleasure as she tongued me. The thought that serving me was turning her on just made my pleasure all the sweeter

It didn't take long for me to come. With Sandy's fingers curled inside of me and her tongue pressed against my clit I felt the tremors coming over me within a few minutes. My knees felt weak and my whole body shook as waves of pleasure ran through it, each emanating from the place where her mouth pressed against me. I pushed her into me even harder.

"That's it, slut. That's right. You're going to make me come. Good girl. Oh, good girl. That's it. That's..." And then there were no more words. I was coming, long and hard. I could feel the pulse beating in my cunt, the explosions of pleasure in my stomach. I gripped Sandy's hair so tight it made her squeal, and even that was pleasure for me. Wave after wave of it. I bit my lip to keep from crying out. My toes curled inside my shoes. My heart pounded.

And then at last it was over. I released Sandy, and slowly eased my panties back into place. I let me skirt drop. I was still feeling a little faraway and floaty from the orgasm, but I had enough presence of mind to gesture for Sandy to stand. With her on her feet once more we looked perfectly ordinary. Nobody would know that anything unusual had happened.

"That," I said, "was just what I needed."

"Did I do okay?" said Sandy. She brushed a stray hair back behind her ear. "You enjoyed that, right?"

I smiled and shook my head. "Of course I enjoyed it. And you?"

Sandy nodded enthusiastically. "It felt good. The way you held my hair. The way you pushed me into you. And... um... and I kind of liked the things you were saying. What you were calling me."

"Good," I said. I stepped a little closer, raised a hand and brushed it against Sandy's cheek. "That's just a little taster of what we'll be doing tonight."

"Oh, I can't wait," said Sandy. She bit her lip. "Will I be allowed to come tonight? I've been so turned on since we talked yesterday that I can't concentrate on anything."

"We'll see," I said, my voice steady and calm. How wonderful! How incredible! She was asking for my permission to come already. It couldn't be more clear how excited Sandy was, but just the same I felt like checking. With a quick glance towards the door to make sure we were alone I reached forward and lifted Sandy's skirt. My other hand cupped her through her tights and panties, and felt the warmth emanating from her, the wetness soaking through. Sandy groaned and pressed forward into my touch. She was so horny I could practically smell it.

Well, good. Patience was something I wanted her to learn.

"Please," she whispered. I put a finger against her lips.

"Tonight," I said. And then I removed my other hand from her crotch and let her skirt fall back into place. "Wait here for five minutes then come back down," I ordered. "Bring some files with you so that it looks like you were doing something up here. Understand?"

Sandy gave me a melting look, a pleading look. I knew that she wanted nothing more than to be touched, to be held, to be fucked. But for that she would have to wait.

"Understand?" I repeated.

She nodded, and I turned and swept from the room without a backward glance. As I resumed my seat at my desk downstairs my whole body was still glowing from the energy of my secret, stolen orgasm.

*

Despite my little break in the routine, the rest of the day still passed slowly. I spent the time dividing my attention between Sandy and the clock. Sandy herself worked diligently through the day – at least when she knew I was watching her she did. As soon as she thought that I was looking away she'd be stealing glances my way, peering over and biting her lip.

I could only imagine the thoughts that must be running through her head. From the sound of what she'd said last night this would be her first BDSM experience. I knew how intense that must be, how turned on she must be. To be honest it was amazing that she managed to get any work done at all.

We'd agreed the previous day that we didn't want anyone at work to see us leaving together. I left a few minutes before five o' clock, saying only a casual goodbye to Sandy – like I would to any colleague. She knew which tube stop was mine, and I'd arranged to meet her outside my building. In all respects it was a perfectly ordinary commute, but the thought of what was waiting for me at the other end meant that I could barely focus on getting off at the right stop.

I arrived at my building and took a seat on the stairs. There was nobody about, much to my relief, and after a few minutes I saw the shape of Sandy's body through the frosted glass of the side door. I hopped up and let her in before she could even figure out which buzzer to press.

"I'm in the right place, then?" she said.

"Yes," I said. "Very definitely." And then I kissed her full on the mouth. She wrapped her arms around me and kissed me back, ardently. For a moment there was no sound in the stairwell apart from our collective breath, apart from the wet sounds of our lips and tongues. Then we pulled apart. "Upstairs," I said. "I want you. Now."

"Yes," said Sandy. And she hurried upstairs ahead of me. I followed her, watching the way her legs moved beneath her skirt. Oh, she was fine. I couldn't believe how lucky I was – not just to have found her, but to have my desires reciprocated. She could so easily have been straight, so easily have been vanilla. I truly was a very lucky woman.

I let Sandy into my apartment, and she entered with some degree of caution. I couldn't blame her. If I was her my mind would be filled with all sorts of questions as to what was in store for me that evening. But, at least for the moment, my apartment was a perfectly ordinary place. There was nothing untoward to see; just my furniture, the prints on my walls, the surfaces of my kitchen counter. Sandy put her handbag down on the little table by the door.

"May I have a drink?" she said.

"Of course." I kissed her briefly, then went to the sink and drew her a glass of water. She drank deeply and then held it in front of her. She was beautiful, standing there. A picture of innocence and vulnerability. "So..." she said, and let the syllable hang in the air.

"So," I replied. I let her take another sip from her glass of water, then stepped forward and took it from her, setting it down on the counter. I grabbed her arm and lead her gently into the middle of the room, in front of my sofa. She came willingly, and then stood there with her arms folded. "Put your hands behind your back," I said. "Let me look at you."

She did so, and I took in her body – not for the first time. It was slender and toned, the breasts just the right size, her face smooth but inquisitive, her eyes bright. Just looking at her was enough to start a pulse beating in my thigh. But I wanted more. I wanted to see what was underneath those clothes.

"Take off your blouse," I said calmly. Sandy obeyed without hesitation, fumbling a little with the buttons. She unfastened it all the way down, and then shrugged her sleek shoulders out and dropped it on the floor. The bra beneath was silken and fringed with lace. I admired the way it cupped her breasts. "Now your skirt," I said. "And your tights." She unfastened the skirt and stepped out of it, and then rolled her tights down her legs and removed those too. Her panties matched her bra – black silk with red highlights. I could see already that they were wet. Sandy resumed her position, standing with her hands behind her back.

I took my time looking at her. I walked all the way around and examined her body from every angle. She was so toned, so pert, so smooth. She seemed almost entirely without blemish or scar. And her hair... the way it laid against her pale skin took my breath away. I couldn't wait to touch her, to play with her. But I would deny myself a little longer, and the denial would make my fulfilment all the sweeter when it finally came.

I stopped behind Sandy. "You want me to touch you, don't you?" I said. "That's what you've been wanting all day?"

"It is," replied Sandy. "Please." She began to turn around, but stopped when I spoke.

"Stay still unless I tell you to move," I said sharply. And then in a softer voice, "You want to please me, don't you?"

"Yes. Yes I do."

"You want me to fuck you? Lick you? Put my fingers inside you?"

"Yes. Oh, god, yes."

"You want me to make you my slave? Subdue you? Deny you? Give you everything and take it away again?"

"Oh, Dinah, yes."

"You will do as I tell you? You will give everything you have to please me?"

"I will."

By this time we were both breathing pretty heavily. We hadn't touched – only words had passed between us, and yet I was so turned on I could barely move. I felt as though I was floating.

"Go through to the bedroom," I said. I followed her through, close behind. So close I could almost feel her warmth. "Stand facing the bed. Put your hands behind your back."

She did so, and I felt a thrill of power at her obedience. I'd put my box of toys on my dresser, which was beside the door. I opened it now and selected a silken blindfold, which I pulled over Sandy's eyes with deliberate gentleness. My hands brushed against her cheeks, but still we had barely touched. She gasped lightly as her sight was taken away from her, and I enjoyed the sound.

Next I removed her bra. The clasps came undone easily and it slipped off over her shoulders. I took a moment to appreciate its satiny feel, then discarded it on the floor. After putting them in

17

front of her to allow me to remove her bra, Sandy returned her hands to their place behind her back. Good. She was learning. I stripped off my own top and bra and then pressed myself against her, wrapped my arms around her body and cupped the pleasant weight of her breasts, one in each hand. She moaned. Her body shivered against me, and I felt every tiny movement. Skin on skin. My fingers found her nipples.

"I will give you pleasure," I whispered in her ear. "As well as pain." On the final word I pinched hard and twisted. Sandy yelped, and began to pull away from me, but I held her firmly in place. "You will take both. You will ask for both. Beg for both."

"Yes," whispered Sandy, and I could hear something like a whimper of pain in her voice, albeit suffused with arousal. Just what I wanted to hear. I pinched and twisted her nipples again, and enjoyed the feeling of tension that ran through her. This time, however, she didn't pull away. I let my hands roam lower, exploring her flat stomach and the waistband of her panties.

"Take these off," I said. I held her arm as, blindly, Sandy peeled away her panties and stepped out of their delicate fretwork. Beneath, I was excited to see, she was almost completely shaved, only a thin strip of downy hair remaining above her sex. Beautiful to see. I longed to touch her there, to feel the contours of her most intimate parts. She stood before me once more, her hands behind her back, my arms around her.

I took a deep breath, and then gently pushed her forwards. She stumbled a little, but I was there to keep her from falling as I lowered her onto the bed. She rolled over onto her back, her hands grasping the covers. I knelt on the bed beside her. All I wanted to do in that moment was to pin her down and feast on her, but I restrained myself.

"Spread your legs," I said. "And put your hands above your head." I watched as she moved herself into the position I dictated. How glorious to see her obey. How beautiful she looked once she had. I got up just long enough to fetch some rope from my box of toys. I held it in a bundle in my hand and let the ends of it trail against her skin. Sandy shivered and arched against the bed. So responsive. I found the end of the rope and held it in my hand.

I tied her right wrist first, making the bond secure but not so tight that it would cut into her delicate flesh. Then I ran the rope under the bed and tied her left wrist, pulling it tight so that her arms were spread out on either side of her, pinned against the bed. She made fists at first, then tried to grab the rope. I watched her struggled with amusement. In this position her chest was bared, her breasts thrust out, ready to be tasted or teased or tortured by me as I willed.

Next it was time to secure her legs. I used another length of rope for this, and took my time, winding it around and around her slender calves. I made sure to spread them nice and wide as well. As I worked I glanced at her sex. It was small and pink and glossy with moisture. It looked like some delicate flower shining with dew. Soon enough I would taste it. Soon enough.

Once Sandy was securely in place I took the opportunity to remove the rest of my clothes. Standing there naked with a naked girl tied to my bed... there was no better place to be in the world, in my opinion. I watched Sandy writhe for a while, testing the strength of her bonds. I knew that she wouldn't escape, but I didn't speak, didn't move. I stayed completely still and silent so that the blindfolded Sandy wouldn't know where I was, or even that I was still there at all.

At last, after much struggling, she fell still. She turned her head from side to side, clearly listening out, trying to detect if I was still in the room. I let her try. She opened her mouth. "Dinah," she whispered, clearly frightened that she had been abandoned.

When I moved, I moved quickly. I stepped forward, sank one knee into the bed and seized Sandy by the throat. I didn't apply much pressure, but I didn't have to. It had the desired effect. Her hands jerked against their restraints, and she gave a high-pitched, panicked gasp. I squeezed a little and she wriggled, trying to get free, panting, her breasts heaving.

"You're mine," I said.

"Yes," whispered Sandy, her voice husky from the pressure on her throat.

"Good girl," I said. Then I put my free hand between her legs and squeezed there too. She was wet. Her wetness soaked my fingers as they sunk into her soft flesh. Almost without any conscious effort I was curling my fingers inside her. She was so wet, so silken, so slippery that I didn't even have to push to be inside her.

For a minute or two I touched her, alternating pressure between her throat and her sex. Squeezing first one and then the other, giving her pleasure and taking it away again. She arched up against me, her body begging for more. I was all too happy to give it to her. Abruptly, I removed both my hands, then retrieved from my box of toys one of my favourite vibrators. It was a Hitachi wand. Battery powered. I pressed the head against her and switched it on.

Sandy moaned as I rocked the head of the vibrator against her. As her noises of pleasure became more strident, I slowly upped the power setting until it was buzzing loudly and she was jerking and twisting against her bonds. Her mouth was open and she was moaning almost constantly. Her whole body shook.

"That's it," I urged. "I want to see you come, right here on my bed. I'm going to make you come. For me. That's it, my slut. Come on. Be good for me."

It didn't take long. Either she was more responsive than I'd thought, or she'd been so turned on that she'd already been pretty close. But within a minute or two she was convulsing against the bed, her cries so loud and so high that become almost screams, her sex spasming, her legs shuddering. Wetness dripped from her and dampened the covers of my bed. I watched her as she came, drinking it all in.

Once her orgasm subsided I removed the vibrator for a minute, and lowered the setting. "That was good, wasn't it?" I said.

"Yes," sighed Sandy. "So good."

"I like seeing you come, my slut. You're going to come again for me now."

And with that I applied the vibrator to her once more. She wriggled and yelped at its touch, but then ground herself against it. I could see in her movements and hear in her voice what it was doing to her, and the thought of such pleasure running through her body turned me on as well. I could have stayed there making her come all day.

I brought her to another orgasm. Again, it was quick, and powerful. She sounded almost as though she were crying when she came, the pleasure so much it sounded unbearable. Just like before, once she'd come, I backed off and allowed her a moment's rest before starting again. The vibrator on low and then slowly going higher, and higher, and higher until she was screaming and writhing once more.

All in all I made her come six times. By the end the patch of wetness beneath had spread and her movements had become weaker. She was panting as though she'd just run a marathon, biting her lip, clutching the ropes. Sweat and wetness shone on her chest. She looked exhausted.

"Please," she cried, when I removed the vibrator after the sixth time. "Please, I can't take anymore."

Smiling, gratified, I switched off the vibrator and laid it down on the bed beside her. Then I straddled her, one leg on either side, my sex in contact with the warm skin of her stomach. Sitting there I began to rock gently against her, enjoying the stimulation.

She felt good, hot and slick and exhausted beneath my body, pinned there helpless, ready to be used and consumed.

"You liked that, didn't you?" I said. "You liked the way I made you come?"

"Yes," said Sandy. "Oh god, I've not felt that good in ages."

"Lovely," I said. "You're so pretty when you come. I could have watched you forever."

"Mmm," moaned Sandy.

"Now though," I said, "it's my turn. I'm going to use you. I'm going to get my pleasure from you. You've going to be my little fucktoy."

"Anything," whispered Sandy. "I'd do anything for you."

"Good girl." I brushed a hand against her sex and it came away dripping wet. I put two fingers in my mouth and closed my eyes, savouring the taste of her, the musky scent that filled my nose. She even tasted good. It was almost too much. I edged up the bead, gripped the headboard in both hands, and then lowered my sex over her face.

Sandy needed no further encouragement. As soon as she felt me pressing against her she began licking and tonguing, straining upwards against her bonds so that she could lick me deeper. Her mouth was hot and eager, and her tongue explored me thoroughly. I let myself press down against her, enjoying the sense of power it gave me. Her hands were tied. Her legs were tied. She was mine to do as I wished with.

I let her lick me until there was a pleasant glow in my stomach, until I could feel the building pressure of a climax coming. Then I fetched another toy from my box – a dildo. It was one of the biggest I owned, thick and full, complete with veins. I mounted Sandy again, this time the other way around. She resumed her tonguing of me, and I bent over her. We were in the perfect position to lick one another to a beautiful orgasm, but instead I licked the tip of the dildo and eased it inside her.

Sandy took it well – it was a tight fit, but she barely moaned at all. I eased it in and out a few time to lubricate the length of it, and after that it moved a little easier. I tilted my hips, and wriggled against Sandy's face. I could feel how wet she was making me down there, how her tongue was edging me towards the brink of a climax. I wanted to fuck her at the same time though, and so I propped myself up on my elbows and started thrusting the dildo in and out of her wet sex.

We were like animals, there on the bed. She was lapping and licking at me like she was starving, while I fucked her steadily harder and harder. She lifted her hips up off the bed with each stroke, urging me deeper, and that in itself turned me on immensely. Her tongue lost itself in the folds of me and I couldn't help but cry out in pleasure.

My orgasm came suddenly. One moment I was simply riding her face, enjoying the sensations of her mouth against me, then next thing I knew I was coming, the pleasure overflowing, a dam bursting inside of me. I let myself go. Completely. Let my wetness flow from me and fill Sandy's mouth, lacquer her face, drench her. She squeaked in surprise, but didn't stop licking. I pushed the dildo home hard, filling her up, fucking her as she made me come. I cried out. I came.

It took me a few minutes to recover from the sweeping power of my orgasm. Once I had, I eased myself from Sandy's face. I was pleased to see that she was drenched in my juices. I watched as she licked her lips, savouring every last taste of me that she could get. I put a hand on her throat again as I removed the dildo from her.

"Good girl," I said. "Good girl. Such pleasure. Time for a little pain, I think."

Sandy nodded. She was still writing weakly against the bed. I could imagine that she must almost be worn out, but I knew that a few sharp strokes from my riding crop would revive her, make her ready again. And then, finally, I would fuck her just as I had longed to since the very moment we met.

I untied her hands and legs, then fetched a pair of fur-lined cuffs and cinched her wrists together. I ran the chain of the cuffs between the slate of the headboard. It was simple, but enough to keep her in place as I punished her. I left the blindfold in place, but after a moment's thought selected a ball gag in addition from my box of toys.

"Open wide," I said. She did so, and I slipped the rubber ball between her teeth. She bit down against it as I cinched the strap tight behind her head. She looked good with her jaw forced wide open, the red of the rubber ball contrasting with her perfectly white teeth. I stoked her hair and her back, then fetched the crop and ran it against her flesh. She arched up into it, as if begging to be punished. Longing for the pain. I pressed the tip against the small of her back and let her feel how hard it was, how whippy, how thin. "You're going to hold still," I said. "No wriggling. No struggling. No trying to escape, you understand? If you move, I'll only hit you harder."

She nodded, unable to speak with the gag fitted firmly between her teeth. I played with her a little longer, running the crop all over her body. Every so often I would raise it into the air and then pause and watch her body tense in expectation of a lash. Then I would return to stroking her once more. She pressed her face into the pillow, clamped her legs tightly together and waited.

At last, when I felt that the moment was right, I delivered the first stroke. I made it hard and fast. The sound of the crop cracking against her skin was music to my ears. Despite the ball gag, she managed to yelp in pain and jerk against the bed. To her credit she didn't move though, simply bore down and waited for the next strike.

24

I delivered the lashes quickly, one after the other, leaving only a moment for the pain to fade. Each time I was rewarded with a yelp, and an involuntary jerk. I could see the tension in her muscles, see how hard it was for her not to try and move away, not to try and shy from the pain. She took the beating. Took every ounce of pain that I gave her. Even before I'd delivered the final lash, a series of thick red welts were rising on her ass.

I paused a moment to admire the marks. While I did, I stroked Sandy's cheek with the tip of the crop. It was something I always loved to do – to intersperse pain and domination with moments of gentle intimacy. Somehow it made the pain all the more striking when it returned. "Almost done," I crooned. "Almost finished. You've been such a good girl, taking your whipping like this. Such a good girl. There'll be a reward for you soon. Perhaps I'll even let you make me come again."

Sandy moaned in assent, and I raised the crop again and brought it swishing down once more, this time without warning, without teasing. I launched myself back into the punishment with even more energy than before. I put everything I had into each stroke, keen for her to feel it, for the pain to last. Perhaps she would even still be feeling it a week from now. Each time she sat down she would be reminded of me, of my domination over her.

I laid into her as hard as I could. And she took it all. By the time I was finished I must have delivered at least twenty or thirty hard lashes. I was out of breath. Beneath me Sandy was sobbing, her ass bruised and welted. I dropped the crop onto the floor and touched her back, ran my hand down her spine to her bruised bottom. She tensed up, but my touch was gentle. The punishment was over now. And what a punishment it had been.

Gently, slowly, I untied her. I lay on the bed beside her and gently removed the ball gag and the blindfold. She blinked, her eyes unused to even the dim light of the room. I drew her face up to mine and kissed her on the mouth, tasting the salt of her tears mingled with the crackle of her saliva. I brushed her wet hair from

25

her face and let her press her shivering body against mine for comfort.

"You did well," I said. "You did beautifully, my slut. You pleased me."

And then, still gently, still tenderly, I guided her head down towards my crotch. She kissed her way down my chest and began licking me once more, though this time it was different from before. Her attentions were slower, more measured, less urgent. Her tongue was languid and easy. It was as if, by punishing her, I had also tamed her. I stroked her hair and put my hand on the back of her neck to pull her into me. Already, I could feel my orgasm building, but I didn't rush or push her. I let her lick me at her own pace, as she wished. Slowly, slowly, the pleasure inside me built until it was towering, until the pressure was almost too much to bear. And then, with Sandy's face pressed against my sex, I let myself go. Let myself come, thrusting and writhing and wriggling on the bed as I did so.

Sandy gripped my hips as my orgasm overwhelmed me. She never stopped tonguing me, never stopped breathing against me. She held me and guided me through the pleasure of my climax, until I was done. Until I lay spent on the bed, worn out, fulfilled, glowing with the aftermath of the pleasure we had shared. Sandy crawled up to lie beside me and I cupped her face, and we tenderly kissed. I'd never felt quite so right in my life before. I was happy. I was satisfied. I held her, and together we drifted off to sleep.

Chapter Three: Going Deeper

The next month followed a simple pattern. Every day I would go into work. Sandy and I would behave towards each other as though we were nothing more than ordinary colleagues. We'd both agreed that our secret was one that we needed to keep between ourselves. To anyone watching there would have been nothing even remotely amiss. We were cordial, polite, sometimes affectionate, but never more so than we might be with anyone else at the office.

After work though, things were different. We always left separately. I would pack up and go a few minutes before Sandy did, and once she'd finished whatever she was doing she would follow me. We took to meeting up at the entrance to my building. Our timings were perfect – I walked slowly from the tube station, and Sandy would almost always catch up with me just as I was letting myself in.

Once inside we would make our way up to my flat. The closer we got the harder it was to keep our hands off one another. We would fall in through the door already kissing, and strip away our clothes in the middle of the living room. Naked, we would pad through to the bedroom. There we would begin to play.

Sandy had to be among the most submissive women I'd ever encountered. That's not to say that she was weak, of course. No. The two are completely different things. If anything she had a very strong personality – which made it all the more powerful and overwhelming that she chose to submit to me.

We would start out by licking one another. After a long day at work with our desires barely kept in check all we wanted to do was sate our needs. I would spread myself on the bed and Sandy would lick me until I came. Then we would move into a sixty-nine position and I would return the favour while sitting astride her face, enjoying the feeling of her breath against my clit.

Once that was done, we would move onto heavier things. I would tie her down and fuck her with my dildo, or with a strap-on. She liked the strap-on. She said it felt as though I really was fucking her when I used it to penetrate her sex. She liked feeling my arms wrapped around her as I thrust it inside. She liked feeling the way my hips slammed into her backside when I took her from behind. And so I would fuck her, long and hard, until she came again and I was satisfied.

Once that was done it was time for pain. Pleasure first, then punishment. That was how we played. I liked to tie her down and whip her, or bend her over my knee to deliver a sound spanking. But we experimented with other methods of punishment as well. I dripped hot wax onto her back, or stretched her ass with some of my larger butt plugs. She was always gagged during her punishments – something she repeatedly told me that she loved.

"It makes the pain easier to take," she said, "when I've got something to bite down on. And when I know I can't cry out."

Sometimes I would even scratch her back with my nails, or with the tip of a knife. We discovered that she enjoyed the layering of these punishments. Hot wax over fresh scratches was her favourite. Or having a butt plug inserted and then being bent over the bed and spanked with a belt. Though she yelped and twitched and often cried at the pain, she never once disobeyed, never once tried to move away from a punishment, never once slipped her bonds.

After the punishment we would pleasure each other once more. Sometimes I thought those were my favourite times. When she had been softened somewhat – her pleasure sated, her body punished. She was always so languid after that, and I always found it so easy to come. I only had to think back over what we'd spent the last hour or so doing and I would already be on the edge. Within a week she had become adept at making me come. She knew just the right amount of pressure, just the right way to use her fingers, just the right way to lick me.

She was perfect. So absolutely perfect. And I told her so as we lay together in my bed after our exertions were done. I stroked her face and stared into her eyes. "You're exquisite," I said to her. She bowed her head.

"Thank you Mistress," she said. That was what she called me now – in the bedroom at least. At work, of course, we remained Dinah and Sandy, but in the privacy of my own home I was Mistress and she was Slut.

*

It was about a month and a half after we first fucked that I decided to take her to a dungeon. We'd spent a lot of time talking about her various fantasies, and among them was to visit a playspace, and be used and pleasured in front of an audience. Well, I knew exactly the right place to make that happen – I'd been there often enough with my old male submissives. Not only that, but there was a party coming up – one which many of my friends would be attending. The other fantasy that Sandy had mentioned to me was a little more complicated: she wanted to be given away, loaned out to be used by men she didn't know.

"I like the idea of just not having a choice," she said. "I trust you. I trust you to make that choice for me. I want to just... be used. Hard. And long. I want to be a toy, a slave, an object."

Well, the party would be the perfect place to make that happen. I floated the idea to Sandy one day as we lay in bed together at the end of a long and glorious session. She lay there in my arms and listened carefully as I told her my idea, the expression on her face unreadable. When I finished she lay in silence for a moment before speaking.

"So... these men... you know them, right? They wouldn't be... strangers?"

I laughed. "Of course," I said. "They'll be strangers to you, certainly, but do you think I'd let someone I didn't know and trust use you? Do you think I'd let someone who I wasn't sure was safe fuck you?"

Sandy rolled over and kissed me on the lips. In turn I rolled over and pushed her down onto the bed, and kissed her back. She smiled, her blonde hair fanned out around her. She always looked so beautiful in bed, so smooth and curved and graceful. Nakedness was a natural state for her.

"I don't think that at all," said Sandy. "I trust you. Absolutely. You know that." She bit her lip. "I... I like the idea," she said. "No... actually, I love the idea. It just makes me nervous as well. It makes me... excited."

I stayed silent and let her think. Eventually she shifted beneath me, looked me in the eyes and nodded.

"You'll come?" I said, quietly ecstatic.

"Yes," said Sandy, still looking me dead in the eye. "In fact, I can hardly wait."

And that was that. All that was left was to organise things. I sent emails to a couple of male friends I'd made over the years, asking if they would be attending the next play party at the dungeon, and if they might be interested in Sandy if so. I included a photo of her on her knees, naked and staring up at the camera. We'd taken a number of photographs, and that one was our favourite. The responses that came in were quick and enthusiastic. Every single one a yes. To be honest, I wasn't surprised. What man would turn down the opportunity to play with Sandy? She was gorgeous. All the same, the obvious excitement thrilled me. It filled me with pleasure to know that she was something to be desired, and that I had her. More than that –

that I would be able to share her, show her off, let others taste the pleasure that was mine to be had at any time I chose.

I told Sandy this. We talked often about the upcoming party, and our conversations got steadily more fevered as time went on. It was plain to me how much the idea of being shared appealed to her, how much it turned her on. And her excitement excited me. We fed off each other, like flame fuelling flame.

"I can't wait to see their hands all over you," I whispered to her one evening as she kneeled beside my bed, her face buried in my crotch. I teased at her hair with the tips of my fingers. "I want to see them ravage you. I want to watch them come in your mouth. Force their cocks into your tight little hole. I want to see you take two at once. God, that would make me feel so good."

Sandy moaned in assent, the sound sending little vibrations through me that only increased my pleasure. I wound her hair around my hand and pressed her face deeper into me, enjoying the way that he tonguing became more frantic and more desperate the more pressure I exerted.

"I can't wait to see you displayed. To see how much your little body turns people on. To see how much they desire you. God, that's going to be beautiful. Watching how you make them horny and knowing that after they've had their fun with you it's me who gets to take you home. Me who gets to possess you."

She moaned again, and I felt drips of mingled saliva and wetness run down my inner thigh. I felt myself brinking, my sex going into spasm, the muscles in my abdomen tightening as my climax came over me. I pressed Sandy's face firmly into me and cried out as I came. II let myself go again, let my fluids flood out of me, let them drench her face and fill her mouth and drip down her body. Again and again I squirted onto her. I shook and shuddered and rocked my hips against her face.

When I was finally done I helped Sandy up onto the bed beside me and we lay together, entangled and panting, slowly regaining our breath. She put a hand flat on my chest in between my breasts and I knew that she was feeling the rhythm of my breathing, the rhythm of my heartbeat.

"I can't wait for you to give me away," she whispered. "I can't wait to be used, hard. All I want is for you to see me being fucked. All I want is for that to please you."

I held her tightly. "It will please me," I said quietly. "It will please me very much."

Chapter Four: The Ultimate Fantasy

It seemed to take ages for the day of the party to arrive, but at last it did. The dungeon was on the edge of town, in a converted stable block in the grounds of a big old hotel. I'd been a number of times, and I knew the owner well. I'd started out by attending parties there on a regular basis, bringing along one or two of my male submissives each time. Very quickly I'd become well-known. What can I say? I was young, I was attractive, and – when I was in my full-on domme mode - I wass really quite impressive.

Very quickly I made a circle of good friends. Not just submissive men either, but a bunch of other dominants who admire my handiwork, and were all too happy to admire a job well-done, or even lend a hand if that was what was needed.

For Sandy I'd lined up three men. One, in the end, couldn't make it to the party, but the other two were definitely up for the idea. One was named Saul – he was a stocky and muscular young man with a shaved head and a couple of tattoos that crawled across his arms and up the side of his neck. The other was named Damien. He was a much-admired dominant, and I couldn't deny that he was certainly very attractive. He was never short of female attention, that was for certain. With his long hair and his strong jaw I could certainly see why. Me and him had very nearly been an item at one stage, but unfortunately it had never quite happened. We were just both too dominant to really get with one another. The wrong energy. That didn't stop me admiring him though, and if I couldn't have him myself, then seeing him use and violate Sandy would be a pleasurable alternative.

So it's safe to say that I was looking forward t the occasion. On the day of the party, work dragged out forever. I found myself glancing constantly at the clock, forever unable to believe that the hour hand had only crawled another millimetre or so in the time

I'd been looking away. The evening seemed an age away, and throughout the whole long wait Sandy was there, tormenting me with her luscious body, untouchable even though she was sat so close.

There was nothing for it, I decided. We would have to take another trip upstairs to the archives. I simply couldn't wait all day to have her.

Just after lunchtime I rose from my desk and beckoned to Sandy. She smiled tightly at me and stood from her seat, smoothing her dress down over her legs as she did so. She followed me across the office, one step behind, and then hurried forward to open the door for me before falling into step once again as we ascended the stairs. We could read each other so well now that there was no need for words.

To my delight the archives were empty. I strode in, and we made our way to the private little corner that was our own. It took only a look from me to have Sandy on her knees in front of me, her head raised, her mouth open. I smiled. I hitched up my skirt and pulled my panties aside, and she applied her mouth to me.

As she licked me I had to admire how good she had gotten over the last few weeks. She'd licked me to orgasm almost every day in that time, and she knew now exactly how to make me come. She no longer even used her hands unless I requested – instead keeping them crossed behind her back. With only her tongue she could bring me to the greatest heights of ecstasy within a couple of minutes. And on this occasion, that was exactly what she did.

I didn't speak as she lapped at me. There was no sound except for our breath, our little moans. I felt the pressure increasing, but I held back for as long as I possibly could. I tightened myself, and let her lick some more. I gritted my teeth. I tensed. When it came the orgasm that swept through me was explosive. My legs shuddered and I almost fell to the floor. Waves of hot, slow pleasure radiated up through me like the tremors of an earthquake. I pushed her face into my wet slid and thrust against her, loving every second of it. She arched her back, her breath hot against my tingling sex.

In the aftermath of the climax I held Sandy's face against me, enjoying the sensation of her breath and her warm body. Then I let her go, and she smiled up at me with a face glazed by my own juices. I drew her up into a long embrace, where I cleaned her, first with my tongue and then with my fingers.

"I couldn't wait until tonight," I whispered in her ear, and she squirmed against me. I could tell that she was horny too, but I put a hand on her abdomen and held her still. "You, however, will wait," I said. "You'll show me what a good, patient little slut you are."

And with that we returned to our office. I worked the rest of the day feeling warm and pleasurable and relaxed, my immediate hunger sated, though I was still ravenous for what was to come.

*

We spent a lot of time getting ready that evening. I had my clothes already picked out, but Sandy was another matter. She didn't own any fetishwear, but I'd selected a few items for her to try and laid them out on my bed. When she arrived at my flat we went straight into the bedroom and she tried them on. My favourite was a little black outfit consisting of a tight bra and a garter belt – it left her slit open and accessible, and it really accentuated the smooth curves of her body.

In fact, I like it so much that I couldn't resist stripping off, lying down on the bed and having Sandy lick me again while she wore it. I had her straddle my face as she did so, so that I could – every so often – take a little taste of her juices, or let her feel the hot stimulation of my breath. No matter how much she writhed against me or moaned or silently begged to be allowed to come, I didn't lick her though. I wanted all her pleasure to be saved for that evening, all her energy to be spent later on rather than now.

Not only that, but I was actually rather enjoying denying her. The longer it went on for the more wet and desperate and horny she became. I deliberately held back until she was all but dripping into my mouth, then finally allowed myself to come, clutching her thighs as I did so. It was exquisite, absolute, pleasure beyond words.

Afterwards, Sandy climbed off me and we tidied up our respective outfits. There was just time for a long kissing session, during which we ran our hands all over one another's bodies – then it was time to wrap ourselves in long coats and pile into a taxi outside my flat.

We behaved ourselves during the journey, but as we climbed out I decided that our driver should be given a little tip. I glanced up and down the street. Night had just fallen and we were more or less alone – certainly nobody close enough to see what was about to happen. I grabbed Sandy and pulled her in front of me, making sure the taxi driver was looking as I did so. Then I quickly and deftly undid her coat and spread it wide open, allowing him to see her almost-naked body beneath.

The taxi driver was pretty cool about it. I saw his eyes widen, and he took a good long look at Sandy's body, drinking in the shape and smoothness of her. No doubt her costume – skimpy as it was – sent his imagination into overdrive. Good. After a moment or two I allowed Sandy to pull her coat shut and the two of us – giggling madly – turned our backs and made our way towards the stable block.

I enjoyed showing Sandy around the dungeon. It was her first time, although we'd talked plenty about what we were likely to see there, and even tried many of them ourselves. Nonetheless it was a rather new experience for her to be in a place where people were playing with an audience, and where the normal rules that govern society seemed to be just a little bit relaxed.

The setup of the dungeon was simple. There was a large room at one end containing a bar and several sofas, tables and chairs. It was a space for people to relax in, although along one wall was a huge rack of toys to be loaned out. The main dungeon was inside the stables itself – each stall had been converted into a different area. On one there were a couple of women engaging in some needle play, while in another a man was locked inside a cage. In a third a woman lay on a leather bed, while a man ran a violet wand over her skin, the electricity crackling between it and her, making her cry out and wriggle and sigh.

After watching a couple of scenes from a respectful distance we went through to the bar area and I got Sandy a drink. She held the bottle in both her hands and smiled at me. "Well," I said. "What do you think?"

Her smile broadened. "I love it," she said quietly.

We spent a little time in the bar, saying hello to people I knew. I took great pleasure in introducing Sandy as my Slut, and she seemed to take equal joy in being introduced that way. Each time I said it she would cuddle up a little closer to me, or gently brush her fingers against my arm. I savoured the contact. And I savoured too my sense of ownership over her. I saw a couple of men and women glancing wistfully her way, and I knew that they would give anything to be able to play with her. But they could not. She was mine, and she was going to stay that way.

We met both Saul and Damien as we circulated the bar. I gave them a knowing wink, but didn't say anything to give the game away. When Sandy was fucked later on I wanted it to be by men who were almost strangers to her, and so I merely introduced them as I would any other acquaintance. They were polite to Sandy. Damien made a mock bow and kissed her hand, which made her come over all giggly. I could tell that she found both of them attractive. Little did she know that she would be getting more than a kiss from them later on.

I decided that, before her big scene, Sandy should get to try some public play. We waited until one of the wall-mounted crosses was free, and then I took her hand and lead her into the stall where it stood. She seemed nervous, but willing, eager even. I pushed her gently against the cross and – good as gold – she raised her arms and spread her legs into place, ready to be bound there. I cinched the leather cuffs tight around her limbs, enjoying the sensation of eyes on us, but paying no attention to anyone but Sandy. With a kiss to the back of her neck, I pinned her in place. The cross kept her upright, and spread her too, leaving her back and her backside open and vulnerable.

I had selected a leather flogger from the rack a little earlier, and I brought it into play now. Gently at first I whipped her back and ass, enjoying the sound of the leather falls hitting flesh, enjoying the way she squealed and squirmed, but was unable to truly move. As the flogging went on, I increased my pace and the power I put into each stroke, and her skin began to redden. Marks appeared there, coming up through her pale skin. They criss-crossed and layered. I paused and licked the red flesh of her back. It was hot, radiating heat. Oh, how delicious.

I flogged her a little longer, until she was practically shivering under each and every blow. Then I fetched a pinwheel from my handbag and ran it tenderly over the red skin on her back. The points of the pinwheel dug into her flesh – flesh that was already sensitive from the whipping it had received. Sandy bit her lip and writhed and clutched at her bonds. She arched her back towards me, and then sharply pulled away. I enjoyed every little second of it.

At last, once I'd played for long enough, I leaned in close to her and whispered. "Are you ready? It's almost time for you to be fucked. Are you ready and horny for me, Slut? Tell me that you are."

She nodded. "I am," she managed, her voice barely above a whisper.

I released her from the cross, and let her heavy body rest against me. I helped her over to a low bench and had her kneel beside it, her body lying flat against the surface. It was the perfect place – it left both her sex and her mouth accessible, and it was easy for people to watch from the entrance of the stall. Saul and Damien were both watching already, along with a handful of admiring others. I felt a sense of pride as their eyes roamed across me and my slut. They were envious of us, eager to use her. There could be no better feeling that that.

I wasn't quite done with Sandy yet though – there was one last thing I wanted to do to her before I let my friends have their way.

From my handbag I removed her favourite butt plug and sachet of lubricant. I balanced the plug on her bag while I opened the sachet and slathered the lubricant all over it, coating its smooth surface in silky white fluid. Sandy knew what was coming, and she bowed her back a little to give me better access to her tight little hole. She gripped the sides of the bench, and I teased the butt plug against her ass. I slipped it in a little way, and let her get used to that, before pushing it gently all the way home. It slipped into place perfectly, and Sandy groaned with pleasure.

I stepped back. There. Perfect. Now she could have all her holes filled at once. I couldn't wait any longer. I bent down and kissed her on the mouth, long and deeply. Then I waved to Saul and Damien, who made their way into the stall. They both looked eager, and could see that they were hard beneath their clothes. Wonderful. I bowed and swept a hand towards Sandy, still bent over the bench. She was watching me sidelong through her hair, her eyes wide. I saw her gaze flick towards the two men who were about to fuck her. There was nervousness there, but there was also hunger.

"Thank you for this," said Saul, with the hint of a smile. "She's a wonderful little gift."

"Enjoy her," I said. "I know she'll enjoy you."

39

I watched as they stripped off. Two muscular bodies and two erect cocks, and Sandy in between them, nearly-naked, bent over and open and vulnerable. It was a dream come true. They circled her, like lions circling prey. I could feel everyone watching, drawn by the intensity of our scene.

Damien was the first to step forward. He took Sandy's mouth. Winding one hand in her hair he pulled her up a little further so that her face was level with his cock. She glance up at him, and then down at his cock, and then – with every sign of eagerness, lunged forward and took it in her mouth. She closed her eyes and sucked firmly, pleasure written in every line of her body. Damien rolled his head back and flexed his shoulders, clearly enjoying her attentions.

I watched Sandy suck him with interest. He was eager but gentle, pushing deep into her mouth, yet she took it easily, without gagging or choking. She was, I realised, really rather talented. I'd never realised. She'd sucked my strap-on before, of course, but a strap-on was no substitute for a real, living cock, and she seemed more than capable when it came to handling the latter. Her hair bobbed around her face, and Damien's cock plunged into and out of her mouth. Her eyes were shut, her body writhing in pleasure.

Then Saul joined in. He knelt behind her and put his hands on either side of her body, steadying her hips. She tilted them towards him, inviting him to penetrate her. He did so gladly, pushing his cock smoothly into her, until his hips were against her backside. For a moment Sandy shuddered between the two men. I recognised the signs at once – the way she shook, the way she flushed, the way a high pitched moan escaped her throat around the gag of Damien's cock. She was coming. I knew it just by looking at her. She was coming hard, all her holes filled, her body exposed. The sight turned me on so much that I wanted to start touching myself then and there, but I resisted, if only just.

The two guys allowed her a moment to herself. Then they started thrusting again. Both of them. Saul was fast and rough, bucking into her in a strong rhythm. Damien was gentler – he held her hair and let her control how deep he went. She was like a doll between them. I watched eagerly. Each thrust from Saul sent a tremor through her body, all the way up to her head, where her lips were wrapped firmly around Damien's cock.

I could have watched them fuck her all day. It was one of the most exciting things I'd ever seen. I moved around the trio, observing from all different angles, before settling on a place just behind Damien and a little to one side. If I stood there it meant that Sandy could see me when she opened her eyes – could even make eye contact with me. This she did, staring at me even as she sucked and was fucked. There was a look of desperation in her eyes, and it was a look I recognised all too well. She wore it whenever she was close to coming, whenever she was right on the edge, and simply needed permission to tip herself over.

Gladly, I gave her permission. "Come for me," I said. And she did. The tremors shook her again, and her skin flushed, and Saul grunted in pleasure – I could imagine that he was feeling the spasms of her sex. Seeing my slut come like that was a joy for me, an unadulterated pleasure. It was an image that I burned into my brain, and would savour for months to come.

It wasn't long before the guys came. Damien finished first. I saw the tension building in the lines of his body, his grip tightening on my slut's hair. And then suddenly he pushed a little deeper into her mouth and arched his back. I watched, fascinated, as Sandy swallowed quickly, her eyes shut, her lips wrapped tight around his cock, not losing a single drop. Her throat bobbed as she swallowed, and I imagined the salty spurts of come disappearing down her throat.

Saul finished before Damien had pulled out. He drove home and I watched as pulse after pulse of shuddering pleasure ran through his body. I could see that he was deep inside her, and I

41

knew that he was pumping her full of his come. The thought excited me beyond words. Sandy herself shuddered in between the two cocks as she was filled. Her face was wracked with ecstasy.

At last, spent, the two men pulled out. Released, Sandy bent back over the bench, panting heavily. Saul and Damien got their clothes back on, and bowed their way out of the stall, giving Sandy back to me. I approached her and put a hand on her back. Her skin was hot and slicked with sweat, and I could feel the flutter of her heartbeat. She was smiling broadly, her eyes shut, floating.

Gently, ever so gently, I turned her over. There was one last thing I wanted – my own satisfaction. She lay on her back on the bench, her breasts cupped by the black silk of her outfit, her groin framed by her garter belt. Already Saul's silky fluid was leaking out of her, and the sight of her used sex thrilled me. It looked wet, debased. I bent over her and kissed her on the mouth, tasting the salty residue of Damien there. Our audience watched on, enthralled, and I felt them drinking in my beautiful body and Sandy's body too.

After kissing her, I quickly worked my way down her body, kissing and tasting the salt on her skin as I went. At her sex I paused and licked, tasting the come leaking out of her, tasting the heat of her, her own juices mixed with those of a man. She'd been well used, and my tender tongue must have felt good after such a fucking. I licked her, savouring her taste, how it mingled with the new flavour of come.

As I licked her I reached up under my skirt and started touching myself. I'd held back for so long that I wasn't far from my climax. I pressed firmly through my panties, then pulled them aside and stroked myself skin on skin. It was heavenly. The tastes in my mouth, the sensations in my belly. Every inch of me tingled with held-in pleasure, waves of it radiating through me from the top of my head to the tips of my toes. I licked more firmly, and as I did so my touch became more firm as well, until I was stroking myself in earnest, becoming feverish as my climax approached.

When it hit me it was like a dam bursting. I cried out and clutched at Sandy's prone body. Her hand found mine and we gripped each other, tight and tender. I came and came, my orgasm rippling through my entire body. Lights flashed behind my eyes. I convulsed. I was nothing but pleasure, nothing but ecstasy.

And then, at last, it was over. Sandy and I lay together, my head against her stomach. I could hear a buzz of voices and other dungeon noises, but they were distant. All that mattered was me and her. It was a long time before we sat up and longer still before we stood. We spent the time kissing. And when we finally rose to our feet and turned to face the watching crowd, we were greeted – by our surprise – by a round of applause.

"They're clapping us," said Sandy vaguely.

I nodded. "Well," I said, "you have to admit that was quite a performance." Sandy nuzzled into me and we made our way out of the dungeon. We would be back though, that was for certain. She was my slut, my own, my slave, and things between us were only just getting started.

Collection Taboo Sex Erotica

www.TabooSexErotica.com

Series: Sex guide

Series: BDSM

Series: Stepmom

Series: Stepdad

Series: Cousin - Cousin

Series: Pleasure Anal Sex

Series: Employee – Boss

Series: Naughty mom

Series: Escort

Series: Lesbian

The Author

Marguerite de Lyon

Marguerite de Lyon is a Paris-born author with a powerful true story of love, heartbreaking betrayal, and a desperate attempt to make a new life for herself.

Marguerite Petite who was born into a family of six other children, one sister, the rest of whom were boys. At the age of 16, her sister was sent by her extremely strict Catholic mother to be a missionary in Africa. After her sister's arrival however, it became known that she was being regularly molested and raped, yet nothing could be done for her and she was never heard from again. Causing major psychological and emotional scarring at a very young age. Determined to not let this nightmare repeat itself, Marguerite found refuge in her first boyfriend Maurice, who she met at the age of 19.

Irresistibly charming, handsome and caring, Marguerite knew Maurice would be the perfect ticket away from her overbearing mother, and she finally vowed to leave her harsh family life behind. She made her escape and never saw her mother or siblings again. Unfortunately, all Marguerite was really doing was trading one harsh master for another. Maurice soon forced Marguerite into a life of prostitution, making her a favorite among French ministers and heads of state, including the prime minister himself. Eventually, she opened "The Abbey," a highly discreet brothel for French elites within the government, as well as ministers, doctors, lawyers and priests who all came to regularly call on Madame Marguerite. Eventually Marguerite came to embrace her life in the sex industry, and turned The Abbey into one of the most elite, exclusive brothels in all of France. In spite of her success, there was always something in the back of her mind that made her wonder if this is what the rest of her life would look like.

Just as suddenly as Marguerite was thrust into the dark world of French prostitution, so was she given an opportunity to flee: a client quietly slipped her a passport, visa and airline ticket for the United States. And so, just as she bravely escaped the iron clutches of her mother as a child, so now she would she once again flee a life of imprisonment and slavery for the New World and another chance at starting over.

Today, Marguerite has two sons and lives in the beautiful city of Carlsbad, California. Sitting in her home not far from the seemingly endless sunny beaches along the Pacific Ocean, Marguerite began recording her life story at the behest of a friend who for years told her she had a duty to use her gift as a wonderful   storyteller.